**Grade 4 Piano**

# Improve your scales!

## Paul Harris

FABER _ff_ MUSIC

# Introduction

**Scales and arpeggios _are_ important. And if taught and learned imaginatively, they can be fun!**

_Improve Your Scales!_ is designed to help you approach scale learning methodically and thoughtfully. Its intention is to turn learning scales into a pleasant, positive and relevant experience by gradually building up the skills to play them through cumulative and enjoyable activities.

**What _Improve Your Scales!_ is about**

The idea of _Improve Your Scales!_ is to present you with lots of engaging activities that lead up to playing the scale (and arpeggio). Actually playing the scale is the last thing that you do! These activities build up an understanding (of the fingering, technical issues, the sound, particular features, sense of key and connections with the pieces that you play) to help make the learning of scales really relevant.

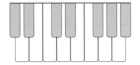

At the top of each scale is a keyboard showing the notes of that particular scale (the minor keys have two keyboards for the melodic minor pattern). This is for you to fill in with whatever you find most useful. Here are some suggestions:
- highlight or colour in the notes of the scale – so you can see the pattern of black and white notes.
- fill in the note names.
- add the fingering you will use for both hands.

Here are two really important **Golden Rules**:

**No 1** Before practising your scales make sure that you:
- Drink some water (this helps get the brain working!)
- Relax (especially shoulders, arms, wrists and fingers)
- Check your posture.

**No 2** Always practise the scale and arpeggio of the pieces you are learning.

**Acknowledgements**

Firstly a big thank you to Diana Jackson who, through her considerable and distinguished teaching experience, has furnished many valuable thoughts and ideas.

Thanks also to Claire Dunham whose terrific eye for detail has been invaluable. Also to my own teacher Graeme Humphrey who helped so much in preparing the first edition, and Ann Priestley for many useful comments.

Finally, huge thanks to Lesley Rutherford, my wonderful editor at Faber Music, who always goes well beyond the call of duty.

# Fingering made easy!

There are only a few fingering patterns used for scales. Once you have these clearly in your mind you'll realise that fingering scales is really easy to master!

Every basic scale (major or minor) has eight notes - but we only have five fingers. So we have to devise simple repetitive patterns that will allow us to play the scales comfortably and fluently. Once you understand the pattern you've virtually learnt to play the scale!

Most of the scales in Grade 4 use finger patterns that you already know. There are just three new patterns to learn (unless you learn both forms of C sharp minor in which case you'll learn four new patterns).

## Right hand

A♭ **major**, both forms of **G♯ minor** and **C♯ harmonic minor** all share this fingering:
23 **123** **1234** **123** **123**

D♭ **major:**
23 **1234** **123** **1234** **12**

C♯ **melodic minor** uses:
23 **1234** **123** **1234** **13** 21 **321** **4321** **321** **32**

## Left hand

A♭ **and** D♭ **majors**, and both forms of **G♯** and **C♯ minors** use:
**321** **4321** **321** **4321** **2**

Think about why these patterns have been devised and why they work well. It will make learning them much more straightforward. For example, in B♭, E♭, A♭ and D♭ majors the thumb will always fall on F and C in the right hand.

## Arpeggios

There are just two finger patterns you will need to know for the arpeggios (with one exception); the basic white note arpeggio pattern:
RH: **123** **1235**
LH: **5(3or4)21** **(3or4)21**

And for all arpeggios that begin on a black note:
RH: 2 **124** **124**
LH: 21 **421** **42**

With the exception of B♭ major left hand which is more comfortable as: **321** **321** **2**

The complete scale and arpeggio are given on pages 25 and 29.

# B♭ major

Fill in the scale:
(See page 2 for details of how to do this.)

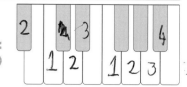

Write the key signature of B♭ major (treble and bass clefs):

The relative minor of B♭ major is: D major
                                        minor

> **TOP TIP** Thumbs are rarely used on black keys in scales, so you'll need to learn some different finger patterns (see page 3).

## Finger fitness

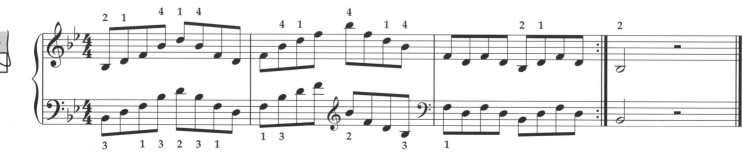

## Key piece    Butterfly

**Have a go**  Using both hands, or just the right-hand line, compose or improvise an answering phrase or a short piece beginning with these notes:

## Sight-reading

**1** In which key is this piece?

**2** Think about the fingering.

**3** What will you count? Tap the rhythm of each line separately, then both lines together.

**4** What patterns can you see in bars 1 (RH), 2 (LH) and 3 (RH)?

**5** Try to hear the music in your head before you begin.

You are now ready to **say** the notes, **hear** the scale or broken chord in your head (playing the keynote first), **think** about the fingering and then **play** the scale and arpeggio with confidence!

# E♭ major

Fill in the scale: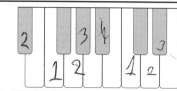

Write the key signature of E♭ major (treble and bass clefs):

The relative minor of E♭ major is: G minor

> **TOP TIP** Remember to practise with even tone and rhythm throughout.

## Finger fitness

## Key piece    Energetic Escapade

**Have a go** Using both hands, or just the right-hand line, compose or improvise an answering phrase or a short piece beginning with these notes:

## Sight-reading

1 In which key is this piece?

2 Can you spot the scale patterns? Are there any repeated rhythmic patterns?

3 What will you count? Tap the rhythm of each line separately then both lines together.

4 How will you convey the character of the piece?

5 Try to hear the music in your head before you begin.

You are now ready to **say** the notes, **hear** the scale or broken chord in your head (playing the keynote first), **think** about the fingering and then **play** the scale and arpeggio with confidence!

The complete scale and arpeggio are given on pages 25 and 29.

# C minor

**Fill in the scale:**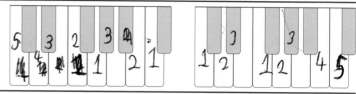

Write the key signature of C minor (treble and bass clefs):

The relative major of C minor is: _____

> **TOP TIP** Although you don't have to use staccato in your scales yet, you may like to include some in your scale practice.

## Finger fitness

### Harmonic exercise

### Melodic exercise

### Arpeggio exercise

## Key piece   Chrysanthemum

**Have a go** Using both hands, or just the right-hand line, compose or improvise an answering phrase or a short piece beginning with these notes:

## Sight-reading

1 In which key is this piece?

2 Can you spot the scale and arpeggio patterns? Which form of the scale is used?

3 What will you count? Tap the rhythm of each line separately then both lines together.

4 What is the character of the piece? How will you convey it?

5 Try to hear the music in your head before you begin.

You are now ready to **say** the notes, **hear** the scale or broken chord in your head (playing the keynote first), **think** about the fingering and then **play** the scale and arpeggio with confidence!

10

The complete scale and arpeggio are given on pages 25 and 29.

# A♭ major

Fill in the scale:

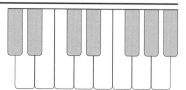

Write the key signature of A♭ major (treble and bass clefs):

The relative minor of A♭ major is: _____

> **TOP TIP** This is the first scale to start with two black notes, which is why we start with 2, 3 (RH) and 3, 2 (LH).

## Finger fitness

**1**
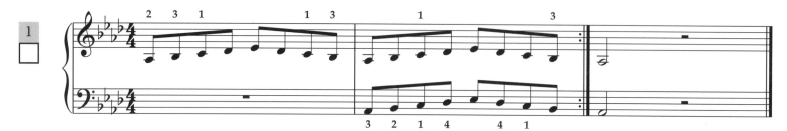

**2**
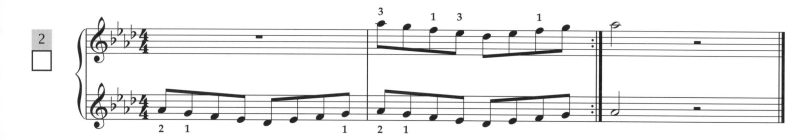

**3**
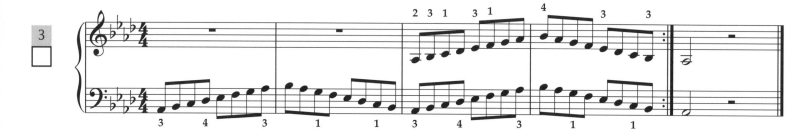

**4**

## Arpeggio exercise

**5**
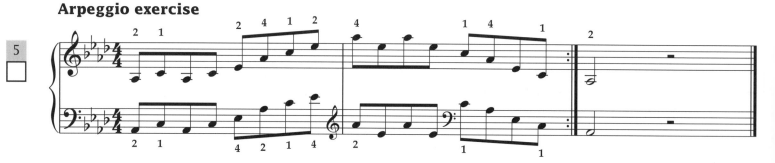

1

# Key piece    Aubade

2

**Have a go**  Using both hands, (you may like to continue the LH idea throughout your piece), or just the right hand line, compose or improvise an answering phrase or a short piece beginning with these notes:

3

# Sight-reading

**1** In which key is this piece?

**2** Can you spot any repeated patterns? And any scale patterns?

**3** What will you count? Tap the rhythm of each line separately then both lines together.

**4** How will you bring character to your performance?

**5** Try to hear the music in your head before you begin.

4

You are now ready to **say** the notes, **hear** the scale or broken chord in your head (playing the keynote first), **think** about the fingering and then **play** the scale and arpeggio with confidence!

The complete scale and arpeggio are given on pages 25 and 29.

# F minor

**Fill in the scale:**

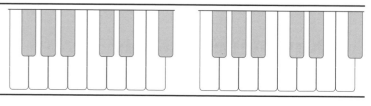

Write the key signature of F minor (treble and bass clefs):

The relative major of F minor is: _____

> **TOP TIP** Notice that F minor uses the same finger pattern as F major.

## Finger fitness

1

## Harmonic exercise

2

## Melodic exercise

3

## Arpeggio exercise

4

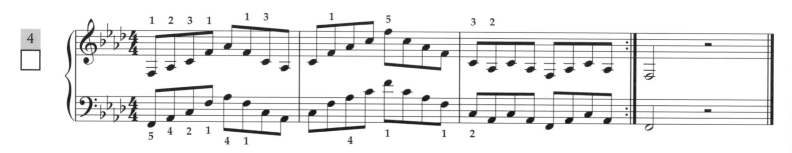

**1**

## Key piece    Fantasy in Five

**2**

> **Have a go** Using both hands, or just the right-hand line, compose or improvise an answering phrase or a short piece beginning with these notes:

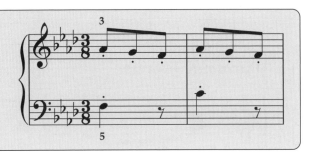

**3**

## Sight-reading

**1** In which key is this piece?

**2** Can you spot the scale and arpeggio patterns?

**3** What will you count? Tap the rhythm of each line separately then both lines together.

**4** What do bars 1 and 2 have in common?

**5** Try to hear the music in your head before you begin.

**4**

> You are now ready to **say** the notes, **hear** the scale or broken chord in your head (playing the keynote first), **think** about the fingering and then **play** the scale and arpeggio with confidence!

The complete scale and arpeggio are given on pages 25 and 29.

# D♭ major

Fill in the scale: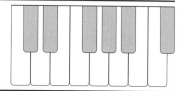

Write the key signature of D♭ major (treble and bass clefs):

The relative minor of D♭ major is: _____

> **TOP TIP** Like B major, this key uses all the black notes, but D♭ major includes the higher of the two white notes each time.

## Finger fitness

1

2

3
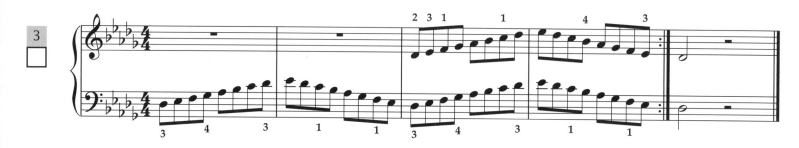

4

### Arpeggio exercise

5

**1**

# Key piece    Dreamy Days

**As if sitting by a cool stream under a leafy tree**

**2**

**Have a go**  Using both hands, or just the right-hand line, compose or improvise an answering phrase or a short piece beginning with these notes:

**3**

# Sight-reading

**1** In which key is this piece?

**2** Can you find the scale patterns?

**3** What will you count? Tap the rhythm of each line separately then both lines together.

**4** How will you bring character to your performance?

**5** Try to hear the music in your head before you begin.

**Espressivo**

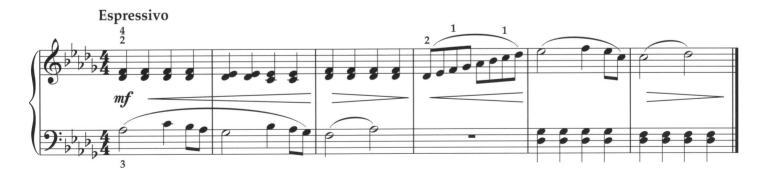

**4**

You are now ready to **say** the notes, **hear** the scale or broken chord in your head (playing the keynote first), **think** about the fingering and then **play** the scale and arpeggio with confidence!

# C♯ minor

Fill in the scale: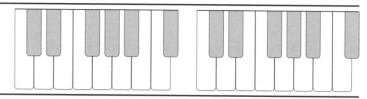

Write the key signature of C♯ minor (treble and bass clefs):

The relative major of C♯ minor is: _____

> **TOP TIP**  In the harmonic version of this scale there is a big gap (6th–7th notes) as we skip from a white to white note, across a white key. Be careful placing your R.H. 4th finger on the D♯.

## Finger fitness

## Harmonic exercise

## Melodic exercise

# Paul Harris'
# Exam
# Workout

## Improve your sight-reading!

**New editions**

The ability to sight-read fluently is an important part of musical training, whether intending to play professionally, or simply for enjoyment. By becoming a good sight-reader, the player will be able to learn pieces more quickly, pianists will accompany more easily and all musicians will play duets and chamber music with confidence and assurance. Also, in grade examinations, a good performance in the sight-reading test will result in useful extra marks!

These completely new editions are designed to help incorporate sight-reading regularly into practice and lessons, and to prepare for the sight-reading test in grade examinations. They offer a progressive series of enjoyable and stimulating stages which, with careful work, should result in considerable improvement from week to week.

Step by step, the player is encouraged to build up a complete picture of each piece. Rhythmic exercises help develop and maintain a steady beat, whilst melodic exercises assist in the recognition of melodic shapes at a glance. The study of a prepared piece with associated questions for the student to answer helps consolidate acquired skills and, finally, a series of real, unprepared sight-reading tests in *Going Solo*.

Now available: two *Improve Your Sight-reading!* Piano duet books which give players a chance to practise their sight-reading skills with another player. Carefully paced to be used alongside the rest of the series.

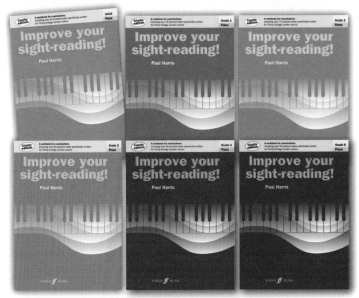

**ABRSM Editions**

| | |
|---|---|
| 0-571-53300-0 | Piano Pre-Grade 1 |
| 0-571-53301-9 | Piano Grade 1 |
| 0-571-53302-7 | Piano Grade 2 |
| 0-571-53303-5 | Piano Grade 3 |
| 0-571-53304-3 | Piano Grade 4 |
| 0-571-53305-1 | Piano Grade 5 |
| 0-571-53306-X | Piano Grade 6 |
| 0-571-53307-8 | Piano Grade 7 |
| 0-571-53308-6 | Piano Grade 8 |
| 0-571-52405-2 | Duets Grades 0–1 |
| 0-571-52406-0 | Duets Grades 2–3 |

**Trinity Editions**

| | |
|---|---|
| 0-571-53750-2 | Piano Grade Initial |
| 0-571-53751-0 | Piano Grade 1 |
| 0-571-53752-9 | Piano Grade 2 |
| 0-571-53753-7 | Piano Grade 3 |
| 0-571-53754-5 | Piano Grade 4 |
| 0-571-53755-3 | Piano Grade 5 |
| 0-571-53825-8 | Electronic Keyboard Initial–Grade 1 |
| 0-571-53826-6 | Electronic Keyboard Grades 2–3 |
| 0-571-53827-4 | Electronic Keyboard Grades 4–5 |

FABER *ff* MUSIC

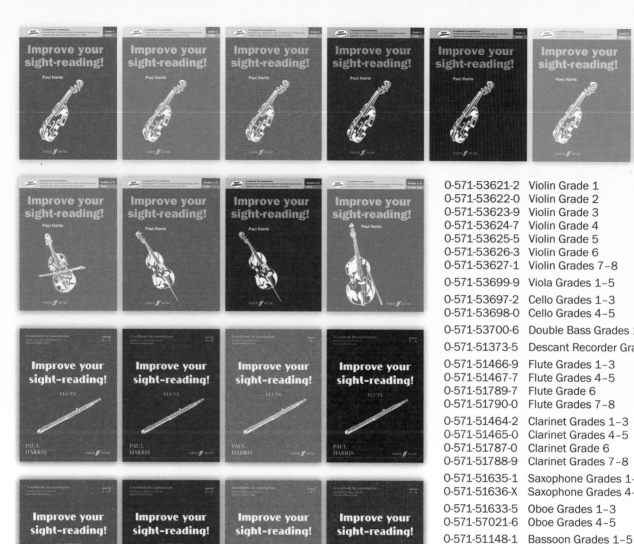

| | |
|---|---|
| 0-571-53621-2 | Violin Grade 1 |
| 0-571-53622-0 | Violin Grade 2 |
| 0-571-53623-9 | Violin Grade 3 |
| 0-571-53624-7 | Violin Grade 4 |
| 0-571-53625-5 | Violin Grade 5 |
| 0-571-53626-3 | Violin Grade 6 |
| 0-571-53627-1 | Violin Grades 7–8 |
| 0-571-53699-9 | Viola Grades 1–5 |
| 0-571-53697-2 | Cello Grades 1–3 |
| 0-571-53698-0 | Cello Grades 4–5 |
| 0-571-53700-6 | Double Bass Grades 1–5 |
| 0-571-51373-5 | Descant Recorder Grades 1–3 |
| 0-571-51466-9 | Flute Grades 1–3 |
| 0-571-51467-7 | Flute Grades 4–5 |
| 0-571-51789-7 | Flute Grade 6 |
| 0-571-51790-0 | Flute Grades 7–8 |
| 0-571-51464-2 | Clarinet Grades 1–3 |
| 0-571-51465-0 | Clarinet Grades 4–5 |
| 0-571-51787-0 | Clarinet Grade 6 |
| 0-571-51788-9 | Clarinet Grades 7–8 |
| 0-571-51635-1 | Saxophone Grades 1–3 |
| 0-571-51636-X | Saxophone Grades 4–5 |
| 0-571-51633-5 | Oboe Grades 1–3 |
| 0-571-57021-6 | Oboe Grades 4–5 |
| 0-571-51148-1 | Bassoon Grades 1–5 |
| 0-571-51076-0 | Horn Grades 1–5 |
| 0-571-50989-4 | Trumpet Grades 1–5 |
| 0-571-51152-X | Trumpet Grades 5–8 |
| 0-571-56860-2 | Trombone Grades 1–5 |

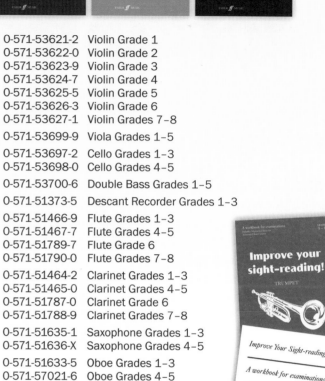

# Improve your aural!

## New editions

The very thought of aural, especially in examinations, strikes fear into the heart of many young pianists and instrumentalists. But aural should not be an occasional optional extra – it's something to be developing all the time, because having a good ear will help improve musicianship more than any other single musical skill.

*Improve your aural!* is designed to take the fear out of aural. Through fun listening activities, boxes to fill in and practice exercises, these workbooks and CDs focus on all the elements of the ABRSM aural tests. Because all aspects of musical training are of course connected, the student will also be singing, clapping, playing their instrument, writing music down, improvising and composing – as well as developing that vital ability to do well at the aural test in grade exams!

| | |
|---|---|
| 0-571-53438-4 | Grade 1 (with CD) |
| 0-571-53439-2 | Grade 2 (with CD) |
| 0-571-53544-5 | Grade 3 (with CD) |
| 0-571-53545-3 | Grade 4 (with CD) |
| 0-571-53546-1 | Grade 5 (with CD) |
| 0-571-53440-6 | Grade 6 (with CD) |
| 0-571-53441-4 | Grades 7–8 (with CD) |

# Improve your practice!

*Improve your practice!* is the essential companion for pianists and instrumentalists, encapsulating Paul Harris's failsafe approach to learning. With boxes for filling in, make-your-own playing cards, a handy practice diary and an exam countdown, these books help to explore pieces and to understand their character. The books will enable the student to develop ways of getting the most out of their practice sessions – whatever their length. Most importantly, the wider musical skills such as aural, theory, sight-reading, improvisation and composition develop alongside, resulting in a more intelligent and all-round musician. Practice makes perfect!

| | |
|---|---|
| 0-571-52844-9 | Piano Beginners |
| 0-571-52261-0 | Piano Grade 1 |
| 0-571-52262-9 | Piano Grade 2 |
| 0-571-52263-7 | Piano Grade 3 |
| 0-571-52264-5 | Piano Grade 4 |
| 0-571-52265-3 | Piano Grade 5 |
| 0-571-52271-8 | Instrumental Grade 1 |
| 0-571-52272-6 | Instrumental Grade 2 |
| 0-571-52273-4 | Instrumental Grade 3 |
| 0-571-52274-2 | Instrumental Grade 4 |
| 0-571-52275-0 | Instrumental Grade 5 |

# Improve your scales!

Paul Harris's *Improve your scales!* series is the only way to learn scales.

These workbooks contain not only the complete scales and arpeggios for the current ABRSM syllabus but also use finger fitness exercises, scale and arpeggio studies, key pieces and simple improvisations to help you play scales and arpeggios with real confidence.

This unique approach encourages the student to understand and play comfortably within in a key, thus helping them pick up those valuable extra marks in exams, as well as promoting a solid basis for the learning of repertoire and for sight-reading.

| | |
|---|---|
| 0-571-53411-2 | Piano Grade 1 |
| 0-571-53412-0 | Piano Grade 2 |
| 0-571-53413-9 | Piano Grade 3 |
| 0-571-53414-7 | Piano Grade 4 |
| 0-571-53415-5 | Piano Grade 5 |
| 0-571-53701-4 | Violin Grade 1 |
| 0-571-53702-2 | Violin Grade 2 |
| 0-571-53703-0 | Violin Grade 3 |
| 0-571-53704-9 | Violin Grade 4 |
| 0-571-53705-7 | Violin Grade 5 |
| 0-571-52024-3 | Flute Grades 1–3 |
| 0-571-52025-1 | Flute Grades 4–5 |
| 0-571-51475-8 | Clarinet Grades 1–3 |
| 0-571-51476-6 | Clarinet Grades 4–5 |

# Improve your teaching!

Energising and inspirational, *Improve your teaching!* and *Teaching Beginners* are 'must have' handbooks for all instrumental and singing teachers. Packed full of comprehensive advice and practical strategies, they offer creative yet accessible solutions to the challenges faced in music education.

*Group Music Teaching in Practice* is a major resource designed to help class teachers, instrumental teachers and music services collaborate and refine their skills to enable them to deliver an holistic primary music curriculum.

These insightful volumes are distilled from years of personal experience and research. In his approachable style, Paul Harris outlines his innovative strategy of 'simultaneous learning' as well as offering advice on lesson preparation, aural and memory work, effective practice and more.

0-571-52534-2   Improve your teaching!
0-571-53175-X   Improve your teaching! Teaching beginners
0-571-53319-1   Group Music Teaching in Practice (with ECD)

# The Virtuoso Teacher

By considering *The Virtuoso Teacher* and how a teacher might attain virtuoso status, renowned educator and writer Paul Harris delves into the core issues of being a teacher and the teaching process. A fascinating look at topics such as self-awareness and the importance of emotional intelligence; getting the best out of pupils; dealing with challenging pupils; asking the right questions; creating a master-plan; taking the stress out of learning and teaching for the right reasons. This seminal book is an inspirational read for all music teachers, encouraging everyone to consider themselves in a new and uplifted light, and transform their teaching.

0-571-53676-X
The Virtuoso Teacher

# The Simultaneous Learning Practice Map Pad

A revolutionary way to set up practice. Take a piece to be practised and write its title in the box; add words to describe the character of the piece underneath. Then set about filling in the significant features in the appropriate bubbles and begin working through these, drawing lines to make connections between them as you go along. You will achieve some really effective Simultaneous Practice!

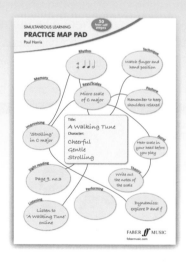

0-571-59731-9
The Simultaneous Learning
Practice Map Pad

FABER ♭♭ MUSIC

Faber Music Ltd.
Burnt Mill
Elizabeth Way
Harlow
Essex
CM20 2HX

t   +44 (0)1279 828982
f   +44 (0)1279 828983
e   sales@fabermusic.com
w   www.fabermusicstore.com
     @fabermusic
     facebook.com/fabermusic

**1**

# Key piece    Chimes

**2**

**Have a go**  Using both hands, or just the right-hand
line, compose or improvise an answering phrase or a
short piece beginning with these notes:

**3**

# Sight-reading

**1** In which key is this piece?

**2** Which form of the minor scale is used?

**3** What will you count? Tap the rhythm of each line separately then both together.

**4** Are there any repeated rhythmic patterns?

**5** Try to hear the music in your head before you begin.

**4**

You are now ready to **say** the notes, **hear** the scale or broken chord in your head (playing
the keynote first), **think** about the fingering and then **play** the scale and arpeggio with
confidence!

The complete scale and arpeggio are given on pages 26 and 29.

# B major

Fill in the scale:

Write the key signature of B major (treble and bass clefs):

The relative minor of B major is: _____

**TOP TIP** Although there are a lot of sharps in this key signature, this is one of the most comfortable scales to play. It uses all the black notes, plus the lower of the 2 white keys each time.

## Finger fitness

## Key piece    Buttercup

**Have a go**  Using both hands, or just the right-hand line, compose or improvise an answering phrase or a short piece beginning with these notes:

## Sight-reading

**1**  In which key is this piece?

**2**  Which notes are not sharpened?

**3**  What will you count? Tap the rhythm of each line separately then both together.

**4**  Where will you have to change hand position?

**5**  Try to hear the music in your head before you begin.

You are now ready to **say** the notes, **hear** the scale or broken chord in your head (playing the keynote first), **think** about the fingering and then **play** the scale and arpeggio with confidence!

The complete scale and arpeggio are given on pages 27 and 29.

# G♯ minor

**Fill in the scale:**

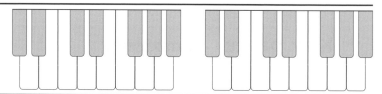

Write the key signature of G♯ minor (treble and bass clefs):

The relative major of G♯ minor is: _____

> **TOP TIP** You may not have come across a double sharp before: ✕. This sign raises a note by two semitones.

## Finger fitness

1

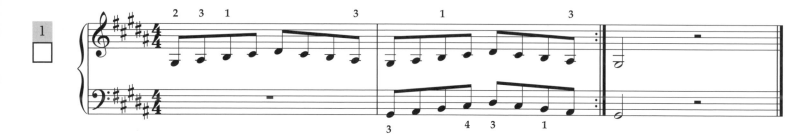

## Harmonic exercise

2

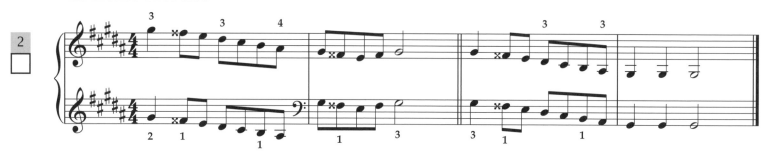

## Melodic exercise

3

4

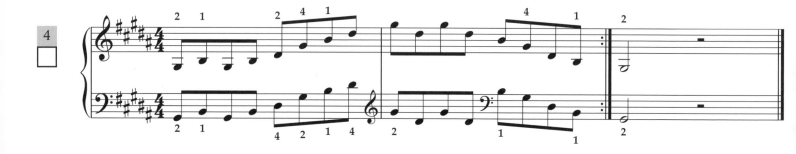

**1**

# Key piece    Gossiping

**2**

**Have a go**  Using both hands, or just the right-hand line, compose or improvise an answering phrase or a short piece beginning with these notes:

**3**

# Sight-reading

**1**  In which key is this piece?

**2**  Can you spot the scale patterns?

**3**  What will you count? Are there any repeated rhythmic patterns?

**4**  Tap the rhythm of each line separately then both lines together.

**5**  Try to hear the music in your head before you begin.

**4**

You are now ready to **say** the notes, **hear** the scale or broken chord in your head (playing the keynote first), **think** about the fingering and then **play** the scale and arpeggio with confidence!

# Contrary motion scale studies

In previous grades, the contrary motion scales have always had the right and left-hand fingers and thumbs coordinating. But things change at Grade 4 – now your hands sometimes have to move independently! So practise hands separately at first, then very slowly when you try them together.

**1**

**Far apart**   Contrary motion scale study using F major

**2**

**Elegance**   Contrary motion scale study using E♭ major

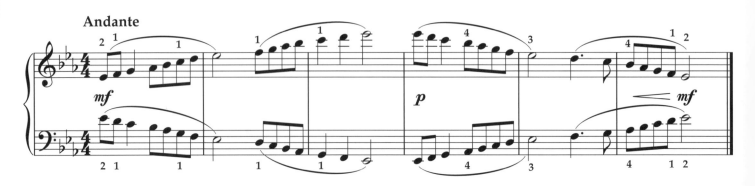

**3**

## Dawn  Contrary motion scale study using D harmonic minor

**TOP TIP** Notice that the big interval comes immediately in the left hand.

**4**

## Crispy  Contrary motion scale study using C harmonic minor

# Chromatic scale studies Starting on a black key

When practising chromatic scales (hands together) use the following pattern:

## Chromatic crunch Chromatic study

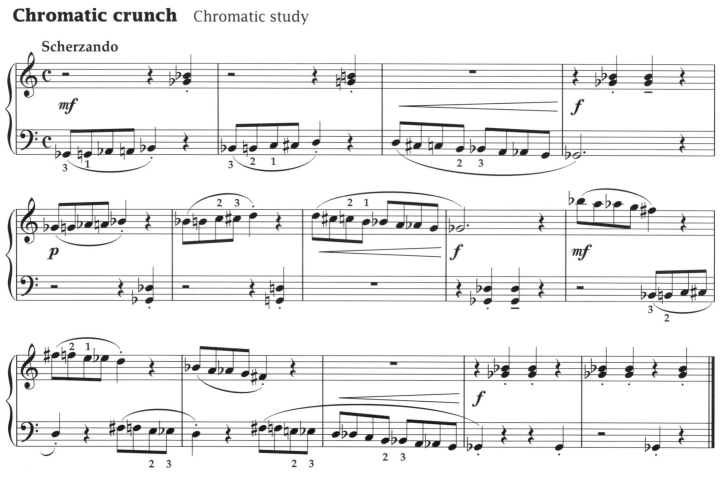

# Complete Grade 4 scales

For Grade 4 exams, the minimum tempo is ♩ = 52. Try practising with a metronome, increasing the speed one notch at a time.

**Exam requirements of the Associated Board:**

- *Scales* major and minor (melodic or harmonic at candidate's choice):
  In similar motion  with hands together one octave apart, and with each hand separately, in the following keys:
  B, B♭, E♭, A♭, D♭ majors (two octaves)
  C♯, G♯, C, F minors (two octaves)

- *Chromatic scales* in similar motion with hands together one octave apart, and with each hand separately, beginning on any black key (two octaves).

- *Contrary motion* with both hands beginning and ending on the key-note (unison), in the keys: F and E♭ majors and D and C harmonic minors (two octaves).

B♭ major

E♭ major

A♭ major

D♭ major

## B major

## C minor harmonic

## C minor melodic

## F minor harmonic

## F minor melodic

## C♯ minor harmonic

## C♯ minor melodic

## G♯ minor harmonic

## G♯ minor melodic

## F contrary motion

**E♭ contrary motion**

**D minor harmonic contrary motion**

**C minor harmonic contrary motion**

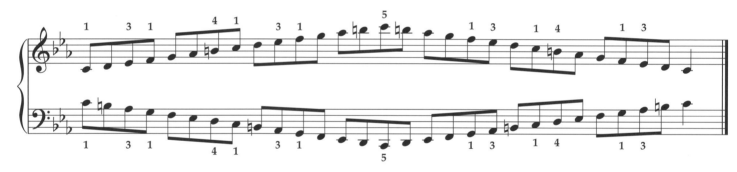

**Chromatic scale (hands separately and together) starting on a black note**

# Complete Grade 4 arpeggios

For Grade 4 exams, the minimum tempo is ♩ = 76. Try practising with a metronome, increasing the speed one notch at a time.

Arpeggios of the *common chords of B, B♭, E♭, A♭, D♭ majors* and *C♯, G♯, C and F minors*, in root position only, hands together and separately (two octaves).

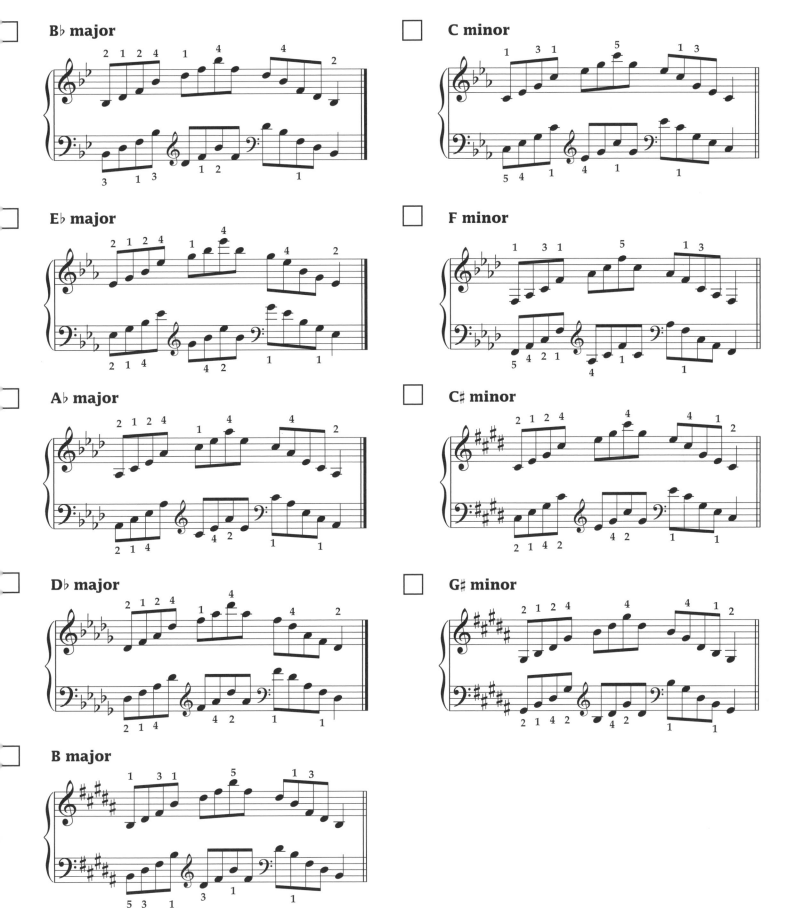

# Practice chart

Remember to practise your scales in different ways – with different
rhythms and dynamics and thinking of different colours and flavours!

| Scale/Arpeggio | Comments | Tick a box each time you practise | | | | | | | | | | | | | | | | | | | | | | | | |
|---|---|---|---|---|---|---|---|---|---|---|---|---|---|---|---|---|---|---|---|---|---|---|---|---|---|---|
| **B♭ major** | | | | | | | | | | | | | | | | | | | | | | | | | | |
| Scale | | | | | | | | | | | | | | | | | | | | | | | | | | |
| Arpeggio | | | | | | | | | | | | | | | | | | | | | | | | | | |
| **E♭ major** | | | | | | | | | | | | | | | | | | | | | | | | | | |
| Scale | | | | | | | | | | | | | | | | | | | | | | | | | | |
| Arpeggio | | | | | | | | | | | | | | | | | | | | | | | | | | |
| **C minor** | | | | | | | | | | | | | | | | | | | | | | | | | | |
| Scale | | | | | | | | | | | | | | | | | | | | | | | | | | |
| Arpeggio | | | | | | | | | | | | | | | | | | | | | | | | | | |
| **A♭ major** | | | | | | | | | | | | | | | | | | | | | | | | | | |
| Scale | | | | | | | | | | | | | | | | | | | | | | | | | | |
| Arpeggio | | | | | | | | | | | | | | | | | | | | | | | | | | |
| **F minor** | | | | | | | | | | | | | | | | | | | | | | | | | | |
| Scale | | | | | | | | | | | | | | | | | | | | | | | | | | |
| Arpeggio | | | | | | | | | | | | | | | | | | | | | | | | | | |
| **D♭ major** | | | | | | | | | | | | | | | | | | | | | | | | | | |
| Scale | | | | | | | | | | | | | | | | | | | | | | | | | | |
| Arpeggio | | | | | | | | | | | | | | | | | | | | | | | | | | |
| **C♯ minor** | | | | | | | | | | | | | | | | | | | | | | | | | | |
| Scale | | | | | | | | | | | | | | | | | | | | | | | | | | |
| Arpeggio | | | | | | | | | | | | | | | | | | | | | | | | | | |
| **B major** | | | | | | | | | | | | | | | | | | | | | | | | | | |
| Scale | | | | | | | | | | | | | | | | | | | | | | | | | | |
| Arpeggio | | | | | | | | | | | | | | | | | | | | | | | | | | |
| **G♯ minor** | | | | | | | | | | | | | | | | | | | | | | | | | | |
| Scale | | | | | | | | | | | | | | | | | | | | | | | | | | |
| Arpeggio | | | | | | | | | | | | | | | | | | | | | | | | | | |

| Scale/Arpeggio | Comments | Tick a box each time you practise | | | | | | | | | | | | |
|---|---|---|---|---|---|---|---|---|---|---|---|---|---|---|
| Contrary motion in F | | | | | | | | | | | | | | |
| Contrary motion in E♭ | | | | | | | | | | | | | | |
| Contrary motion in D harmonic minor | | | | | | | | | | | | | | |
| Contrary motion in C harmonic minor | | | | | | | | | | | | | | |
| Chromatic beginning on any black key | | | | | | | | | | | | | | |

# Why are scales important?

There are many reasons and it's important that pupils know these! Scales will hugely improve all aspects of your finger technique, facility and control.

- Arpeggios will improve your ability to move around the piano with ease.
- Knowing your scales and arpeggios will speed up the learning of new pieces because so much material is usually based on scale and arpeggio patterns.
- Knowing your scales and arpeggios will improve your sight reading both in dealing with technical issues and reading melodic patterns.
- Knowing your scales and arpeggios will develop your sense of key.
- Playing scales and arpeggios well and with confidence will earn good marks in exams.

**Scales and exams**

So that's why scales are an important part of exams! They really do help to develop your playing.  In an exam, the examiner will be listening out for:
- A prompt response
- Evenness of pulse and rhythm
- Control and evenness of tone
- No unnecessary accents
- The smooth passage of the thumb
- A sense of key
- Fluency and dexterity
- A musical shape for each example

Think about each of these during practice sessions. Tick them off in your mind.

© 2010 Faber Music Ltd
First published in 1995 by Faber Music Ltd
Bloomsbury House 74–77 Great Russell Street London WC1B 3DA
Music processed by Donald Thomson
Cover and text designed by Susan Clarke
Printed in England by Caligraving Ltd

ISBN10: 0-571-53414-7
EAN13: 978-0-571-53414-2

To buy Faber Music publications or to find out about the full range of titles available please contact your local music retailer or Faber Music sales enquiries:
Faber Music Ltd, Burnt Mill, Elizabeth Way, Harlow CM20 2HX
Tel: +44 (0) 1279 82 89 82    Fax: +44 (0) 1279 82 89 83
sales@fabermusic.com    fabermusic.com